ACCOUNTABILITY

A guide to accountability-based management
Second Edition

Ginty Burns

www.trafford.com
North America & international
toll-free: 1 888 232 4444 (USA & Canada)
fax: 812 355 4082

What this book is for

This book is a quick and easy reference on the concepts of accountability-based management. You can use it to learn about and apply the principles in your workplace, or to refresh your memory if things seem to be going off the rails.

Who this book is for

Anyone in a business organization who is interested in building a trust-enhancing workplace where people have fulfilling work, are treated fairly, and can count on their manager to add value.

Acknowledgements

Elliott Jaques, for the foundational work on requisite organization.

My colleagues at COREinternational for their support and contributions.

John Bryan (Toronto, ON) for his work on the six levels of participation in decision-making.

Matthew Allen (Toronto, ON) for original artwork.

William Bushell (Victoria, BC) for graphics and cover design.

Web resources

Word definitions: Merriam-Webster Online (www.m-w.com)

Quotations: The Quotations Page (www.quotationspage.com) and Bartleby Books Online (www.bartleby.com)

Biographical information: A&E Television Networks (www.biography.com)

Contents

A is for accountability 2

B is for boundaries.. 6

C is for capability 8

C is also for coaching 10

And C is for collateral teams 11

And C is for commitments.. 12

And C is for consequences.. 14

D is for decision-making authority................................... 16

D is also for delegating work.. 17

E is for employees and employees-once-removed.............. 20

E is also for equilibration... 22

And E is for escalations 23

F is for felt-fair pay 26

F is also for form follows function 28

G is for gap 30

G is also for goals 32

H is for hierarchy 36

I is for individual contributors 38

I is also for information processing capability................... 39

And I is for interdependence 40

J is for jam-up 44

J is also for Jaques.. 46

K is for knowledge.. 50

L is for level of work complexity...................................... 52

M is for manager... 56

M is also for manager-once-removed 57

N is for no surprises, no excuses...................................... 60

O is for output 62

P is for performance 66

P is also for personal effectiveness 67

Q is for QQTR 70

R is for responsibility 74

R is also for rewards and recognition 75

And R is for role clarity 76

And R is for role-person fit.. 78

S is for service providing and receiving.................... 82

S is also for skills.. 84

And S is for span of control...................................... 85

T is for three-tier units.. 88

T is also for timespan of discretion 89

And T is for trust... 91

U is for under-performance 94

V is for values... 96

W is for work 100

X is for cross-boundary relationships....................... 104

Y is for you... 108

Z is for ze glossary and ze end 110

Preface

This book describes how things should work in an organization that uses accountability-based principles. People often say, "But what is an accountability-based company, and how do I know when I've got one?" Well, there are some indicators. It's unlikely all of these will be true, but if most of them are, you are almost there. In an accountability-based company...

- everyone has a sufficiently challenging role that allows them to exercise their creative potential within appropriate boundaries.

- everyone can count on their various vertical and horizontal role relationships to help get their work done by providing what is needed in a timely way.

- managers are called to account not only for their team's results but also for their effectiveness as managerial leaders.

- reward and recognition systems (e.g. compensation, performance evaluation) support the organization's values and business strategy.

- change management and organization design are based on principles, not driven by personality, power, or influence.

- everyone can focus on their own work because they can trust others to do theirs.

- everyone knows what's expected of them and by when.

- there is timely and factual feedback on personal effectiveness.

- everyone can see how they contribute to the organization's goals.

- everyone lives the organization's values.

- there are the right number of management layers.

- every role and level is understood as important and required for success.

- people fit their roles perfectly.

- everyone's accountability is fully matched with authority.

- decisions occur at the right organizational layer.

- work is grouped in a way that minimizes coordination cost, reduces escalation, and eliminates dysfunctional boundary management.

- managers support their direct reports, but don't do their work or tell them how to do it.

- there is fair, non-arbitrary evaluation of everyone's contribution.

- everyone has someone accountable for their development—their manager's manager.

- there is career mentoring for all, not just a select few.

- people feel they are paid fairly.

- there is a belief that everyone is "doing their best."

A is for accountability

Accountable (adj):	subject to giving an account
Account (n):	a statement explaining one's conduct; a statement or exposition of reasons, causes, or motives

Accountability is not the same as responsibility, which is a felt obligation to act within an organization's values (see *Responsibility*, page 74.) Being accountable means you can be called to answer for your own actions and, if you are a manager, for the outputs of your direct reports. The notion of a manager being accountable for his/her direct reports' outputs may seem odd at first, but is logical when you consider that a manager determines the goals for those direct reports, monitors their work, and provides the resources they need to do their work.

In an accountability-based company…

- People understand what they and others are accountable for.

- People get called to account if they do not meet expectations— there are consequences.

"It is not only what we do, but also what we do not do for which we are accountable." (Molière, French actor and comic dramatist, 1622–1673)

Here's what ALL EMPLOYEES are accountable for at all times:

- Their own personal effectiveness (using their best efforts at work)
- Supporting company values and goals
- Working cooperatively with others
- Carrying out assigned work
- Informing their manager if progress on tasks is better or worse than expected
- When in doubt, asking their manager to clarify expectations

MANAGERS are also accountable for the following:

- The work (outputs) their direct reports produce
- The result or impact of their direct reports' behaviour
- Building and sustaining an effective team capable of producing required outputs
- Continually improving processes
- Providing their team with effective managerial leadership, which includes
  - holding regular team meetings
  - setting context for work
  - planning
  - assigning work effectively
  - appraising team members' personal effectiveness
  - carrying out merit reviews
  - coaching
  - selecting and inducting team members
  - when appropriate, initiating a team member's removal from role

And MANAGERS-ONCE-REMOVED (people who manage managers) are also accountable for the following:

- Ensuring their direct reports exercise sound managerial leadership practices
- Establishing work levels and placement in compensation bands for employees-once-removed (employees two levels down, or EoRs)
- Developing a talent pool of EoRs (includes mentoring and career planning)
- Assessing EoRs' current potential and future potential capability
- Planning succession for roles one level down
- Ensuring EoRs are treated fairly and equitably across the organization
- Finalizing their EoRs' placement in/removal from role and, when appropriate, removal from the organization
- Ensuring their EoRs are able to maintain effective cross-boundary relationships

B is for boundaries

Boundary (n):   something (as a line, point, or plane) that indicates or fixes a limit or extent

We all live and work within social, legal, and organizational boundaries. Some boundaries are narrow and restrictive, while some are wide. In an organization, it's important to know where the boundaries of your role are—what you can do yourself and what you have to go to others for. Knowing the boundaries and having the authority to act within them is empowering rather than restrictive.

In an accountability-based company…

- Managers work with their direct reports to clearly define the boundaries around what direct reports can and cannot do.

- People understand their own and others' boundaries and decision-making authorities.

- Managers encourage their direct reports to exercise discretion and creativity within the defined boundaries.

- Boundaries are wide enough to allow people to do their work effectively.

"Freedom is not the absence of structure… but rather a clear structure that enables people to work within established boundaries in an autonomous and creative way." (Erich Fromm, German psychologist and social philosopher, 1900–1980)

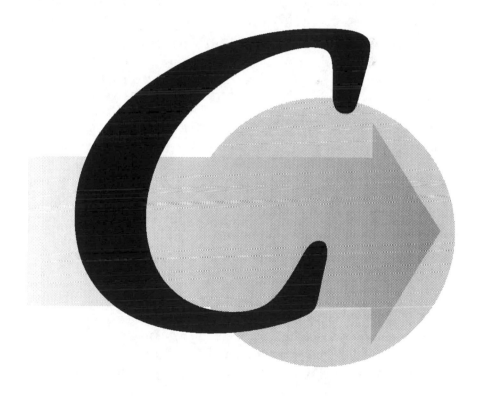

C is for capability

Capable (adj):   having attributes (as physical or mental power) required for
                   performance or accomplishment

Each person's capability to do work grows over time until it reaches
the maximum potential for that person. Someone placed in a job for
which he/she is under- or over-capable at a particular time will be
dissatisfied and may fail, so it's important to match capability to the
job requirements. (See also *Information processing capability*, page 39 and
Level of work complexity, page 52.)

A manager-once-removed (someone who manages managers) is
accountable to assess the capability of employees two levels down,
ensure a proper fit of people to roles, and see that people have
opportunities to grow into more complex roles as they develop.

There are three types of capability:

Current applied capability	the level of work complexity a person is capable of handling right now
Current potential capability	the level of work complexity a person would be capable of handling right now if he/she had some training or a little more experience
Future potential capability	the maximum level of work complexity a person will be able to handle in future

A manager is most interested in a person's current applied capability,
because this is what makes a person effective in their current job. A
manager-once-removed will be interested in assessing an employee-
once-removed's current potential capability and predicting his/her
future potential capability, because these guide a person's career path
and allow for succession planning.

Assessing current applied or current potential capability is not a complicated procedure involving testing and allocation of points. It is a judgment call, where a manager-once-removed and manager review how someone is performing in a particular role by asking these questions:

- Is this person able to do the work of this role right now?

- Does this person solve problems in an appropriate way for the role's current level of work complexity?

- With the right knowledge and skills, would this person be able to do work at the next level up right now? If not now, when?

- With the right knowledge and skills, would this person be able to do work two levels up right now?

- How does this person compare to others in similar roles?

- Does this person do work that, while good, is more than required within the role? (an indicator of over-capability)

In an accountability-based company...

- There is a good match between an individual's capability and the complexity of work in that person's role.

- Managers ensure direct reports have the knowledge and skills to perform effectively in their roles.

- Managers-once-removed are aware of the current and future potential capability of employees two levels down and provide appropriate career development and mentoring to help them reach their potential.

"If your tools are less than what you need, you will expend effort unnecessarily. If they are more than what you need, you will over-invest money, time, and attention to acquire and maintain something that's not worth the effort." (David Allen, American consultant, trainer, and author, 1945–)

C is also for coaching

Coach (v):   to train intensively (as by instruction and demonstration)

Coaching is an important part of a manager's job, because it helps direct reports do their current work more effectively. Anyone who needs coaching is entitled to receive it. Because coaching is related to current work only, it is different from mentoring and career development, both of which are the accountability of a manager-once-removed (see page 57).

In an accountability-based company…

- Managers find out what coaching their direct reports need and provide it at the right time.

- People feel comfortable asking their manager for coaching.

- Managers-once-removed ensure their employees-once-removed receive appropriate coaching from their manager.

"A good coach will make his players see what they can be rather than what they are." (Ara Parasheghian, American football coach)

And C is for collateral teams

Collateral (adj):   serving to support or reinforce; parallel, coordinate, or corresponding in position, order, time, or significance

A collateral team is a team of people who share the same manager.

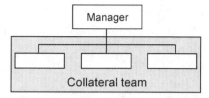

To ensure effective teamwork, it's important for collateral team members to

- understand their own and each other's work and roles.

- differentiate their work as a team from their work as individual team members.

- understand when the team needs to meet, and when the manager needs to be present, in order to get work done effectively.

- manage their relationships so they work well together.

The best way to do all this is through a series of open and honest conversations.

In an accountability-based company...

- Collateral team members share their manager's concern for the overall effectiveness of his/her area.

- Individual team members do what's right for the team and the company as a whole, not just what's right for themselves or their own functional area.

- If in conflict, individual team members think "what would my manager want me/us to do for the good of the team?"

"What we need to do is learn to work in the system, by which I mean that everybody, every team, every platform, every division, every component is there not for individual competitive profit or recognition, but for contribution to the system as a whole on a win-win basis." (W. Edwards Deming, American statistician and management consultant, 1900–1993)

And C is for commitments

Commitment (n):   an agreement or pledge to do something in the future

Many of the conversations that take place in organizations consist of requests and promises (commitments[1]). People who make and keep commitments tend to be trusted, while those who consistently break commitments (whether intentionally or not) lose trust quickly. The following guidelines for accountable conversations help people make clear and genuine commitments:

When making a request:

- Make sure the conversation occurs at an appropriate time, and with the right person.

- Make sure both people are committed to reaching a mutually acceptable outcome.

- Accurately spell out what is required and by when.

- Ensure your understanding of what is required by when is the same as the other person's (by asking the other person to recap).

- Specify your *conditions for satisfaction*—how you will know the commitment has been met.

- Be willing to negotiate if the other person says your request is not possible.

- Make it clear there will be no punishment or arbitrary action if circumstances change and the commitment cannot be kept, but you must be kept informed. Stress the importance of advising you of any change that will affect your conditions for satisfaction.

When responding to a request:

You have three options:

- **Accept** and promise what is requested.

- **Negotiate**—be clear that you cannot promise what is requested, but can offer something else. Continue to negotiate until you can either accept the request or must decline it.

---

[1] Much of this information about commitment management derives from work by John Austin (1911-1960) related to speech acts.

- **Decline**—(after appropriate negotiations) be clear that you cannot promise what is requested and cannot offer anything else.

Once you have accepted a request, make sure you meet your commitment or advise the requestor *immediately* if circumstances change and you think you cannot meet it. This will allow you to make a new commitment, or to escalate (see page 23) if you need your respective managers' help—for example, to provide additional resources.

When a commitment has been met, it's important to *close the loop* by declaring your satisfaction with the outcome. This might be "Thank you: you have delivered what you promised." or "You have delivered something but it doesn't quite meet my expectations." (followed by a constructive conversation about what needs to change and whether or not that is possible).

In an accountability-based company:

- Requestors make clear and reasonable requests, and check for understanding.

- People feel comfortable negotiating requests and offers until a mutually satisfactory outcome can be reached.

- People make genuine commitments by clearly accepting or rejecting a request (after sufficient discussion and negotiation).

- People monitor their commitments and inform the requestor immediately if circumstances change.

- Requestors close the loop on commitments by declaring when their requirements have been met satisfactorily.

- People feel comfortable approaching their managers for extra support if a commitment cannot be made when needed (after appropriate efforts).

"Unless commitment is made, there are only promises and hopes... but no plans."
(Peter Drucker, Austrian-born management writer, 1909–2005)

And C is for consequences

Consequence (n):   something produced by a cause or necessarily following from a set of conditions

Accountability is a function of role clarity, clear task assignments, full commitment to do the work, and the knowledge that *consequences* will be applied according to how well—or not—the work was performed (taking into consideration the conditions under which the work was done).

Often, when people hear the word "consequences," they think of negative ones—not receiving a bonus, or being removed from role. But consequences can also be positive—rewards for work well done.

Positive consequences can be verbal feedback/public recognition (a simple "thank you"), tangible rewards (money, movie tickets, letters of commendation), or opportunities to participate in desirable activities (conferences, training, preferred work). To be effective in driving desired behaviours, rewards must be valued and seen as fair and equitable.

Negative consequences must be seen as fair and consistently applied. Nearly everyone notices if someone who is unsuited to a role is allowed to continue operating in it, or if employees who constantly flout company rules and values are not held to account for their behaviour.

In an accountability-based company:

- Reward systems are well understood, and rewards are valued.

- Managers are accountable to apply both positive and negative consequences.

- Managers provide frequent informal feedback in addition to formal performance reviews.

- Managers-once-removed ensure managers apply consequences (both positive and negative) appropriately and equitably.

- Managers-once-removed ensure appropriate placement of people in roles two levels down and support managers in taking prompt action when an incumbent is not suited to a role.

"There are in nature neither rewards nor punishments; there are consequences."
(Robert Ingersoll, US lawyer, & orator, 1833–1899)

D is for decision-making authority

Decision (n):   a determination arrived at after consideration

Authority (n):   power to influence or command thought, opinion,
                        or behaviour

Decision-making authority is one of the resources a manager grants
to a direct report, and it forms one of a role's boundaries.
Understanding what level of decision-making authority someone has
been granted helps to reduce unnecessary meetings and conflict.
There are six levels of involvement in decision-making:

Be aware   to be informed of a decision before it's implemented

Contribute   to be asked for input before a decision is made

Participate   to participate in discussions before a decision is made

Recommend   to recommend what a decision should be

Decide   to have the authority to decide

Veto   to be able to block a decision

Sometimes people take part in a decision-making process thinking
that they will be recommending or even deciding when, in fact, the
decision-maker only wants their contributions. If you're not clear
what your involvement level is… ask!

In an accountability-based company…

- People know who makes which decisions.

- People have sufficient decision-making authority to carry out
  their work.

- When people meet to make a decision, those with the authority
  to do so are in the room.

- People know when a decision must be escalated, and why.

- People understand the degree of influence they have over
  decisions others make.

- Veto authority is used rarely but appropriately, with full
  understanding of the reasons for its use.

"Nothing is more difficult, and therefore more precious, than to be able to decide."
(Napoleon Bonaparte, French general, consul, and emperor, 1769–1821)

D is also for delegating work

Delegate (v):   to entrust to another; to appoint as one's representative; to assign responsibility or authority

Because the President or CEO of a company cannot do all the work alone, he/she sets up direct report roles and delegates portions of work. Those roles in turn set up other roles, and so on down to the front line. But what work to delegate, and what to keep? The rule is that you delegate as much as you can, as long as it fits within your direct reports' capability (see page 8) and level of work complexity (see page 52), and as long as it's not something you absolutely have to do yourself. For example, a President in an organization with five levels of work complexity will have a longest task of 5–10 years. Not all the President's work will be of this duration—there will be other, shorter-term work that the President must do him/herself, such as giving Board presentations and providing managerial oversight to direct reports. The President can delegate portions of work (with appropriate timespans) to direct reports, and can get support from direct reports to prepare for the Board presentations, but should not delegate the 5–10 year task or the managerial accountabilities: that is abdication! The same principle holds true all the way down the accountability hierarchy.

Guidelines for delegating work:

- Delegate as much as possible, as long as the delegated work falls within the work level and capability of your direct report.

- Set appropriate context for the delegated work.

- Decide and specify if the work output must come back to you once it's completed.

- Be clear about the quantity, quality, time, and resources for delegated work (See *QQTR*, page 70).

- Make sure the direct report understands and commits to doing the work (see *Commitments*, page 12).

- Don't delegate your own managerial accountabilities (see page 3).

In an accountability-based company…

- People understand what their own work is and what they can delegate.

- Managers delegate work clearly, being specific about why it needs to be done, how, with what, and by when.

- People let their manager know if they are unable to take on delegated work—and what would need to change for them to be able to do it.

- Managers don't duplicate work they have delegated to a direct report.

- Managers never delegate their managerial leadership practices (see *Manager*, page 56).

To ensure delegated work is at the right level of complexity for a direct report, ask yourself these questions:

- How long will I give the person to do this task?

- If pressed, would I give the person any longer? What's the longest I could live with?

- Are there stages along the way, where I need to sign off on something before the work can proceed? When would they be?

Then make sure the answer fits with the role's designated level of work complexity:

    Level 1 (0–3 months)
    Level 2 (3–12 months)
    Level 3 (1–2 years)
    Level 4 (2–5 years)
    Level 5 (5–10 years)

"No man will make a great leader who wants to do it all himself or get all the credit." (Andrew Carnegie, Scottish industrialist and philanthropist, 1835–1919)

E is for employees and employees-once-removed

Employee (n):   one employed by another, usually for wages or salary

Employ (v):   to make use of (someone or something inactive); to use advantageously; to use or engage the services of; to provide with a job that pays wages or a salary

Companies need employees in order to achieve their mandate and make their contributions to society. People come to work for many reasons—financial, social, and personal satisfaction—so a company will benefit from providing meaningful, rewarding work, at fair rates of pay, in a trust-enhancing environment. Under these circumstances, employees can be expected to do their best (and can be called to account for not doing so).

Whatever your title (Associate, Team Member, Vice President…) if you receive pay for working in an organization, you are an employee accountable for applying your best efforts to your work. As an employee, you can count on your manager to provide effective managerial leadership, which includes setting context for work, assigning work effectively, appraising your personal effectiveness, carrying out merit reviews, and coaching.

If your manager has a manager, you are that person's employee-once-removed and you can count on your manager-once-removed to ensure you are fairly treated and fairly paid, and help you with career planning if required. (See also *Accountability*, page 2, *Manager*, page 56, *Manager-once-removed*, page 57, and *Three-tier units*, page 88.)

In an accountability-based company…

- Employees feel fairly paid for the work they do.

- Employees feel fairly treated or, if not, can appeal to their manager-once-removed.

- Employees-once-removed have access to their manager-once-removed for career planning.

- Employees experience trust and know that no-one will intentionally do them harm.

- Employees understand and support the company's values.

- All employees, at every level, are valued.

"Most are engaged in business the greater part of their lives, because the soul abhors a vacuum and they have not discovered any continuous employment for man's nobler faculties." (Henry David Thoreau, American writer and poet, 1817–1862)

E is also for equilibration

Equilibrate (v):   to bring into or keep in equilibrium

Equilibrium (n):   a state of intellectual or emotional balance; a state of adjustment between opposing or divergent influences or elements

Equilibration is a process where managers-once-removed (MoRs—see page 57), often with the HR department, ensure that employees-once-removed (EoRs) across the organization are being judged, treated, and paid fairly and equitably; and that the organization's talent pool is assessed and developed.

Managers sometimes find it difficult, at least to begin with, to judge their direct reports' personal effectiveness and determine appropriate consequences or compensation recommendations. Having managers at the next level up evaluate those judgments in light of others that are being made at the same level can alleviate the anxiety and iron out inequities. It also provides information on individual managers' personal effectiveness in carrying out their unique managerial leadership accountabilities.

In a typical equilibration process, managers-once-removed meet at least once a year with their direct report team members to review the assessments their direct reports have made about employees two levels down. They also review information about changes in their EoRs' roles or aspirations, and discuss career or lateral move opportunities for those EoRs.

In an accountability-based company...

- Employees can trust that they will be treated and paid fairly and equitably—there are no "old boy" networks or personal agendas.

- Groups of MoRs evaluate managers (their own direct reports) on how well they carry out their managerial leadership practices.

- MoRs are aware of the career aspirations and capabilities of their EoRs, and do their best to provide development opportunities.

"Equality...is the result of human organization. We are not born equal."
(Hannah Arendt, German-born historian & social philosopher 1906–1975)

And E is for escalations

Escalate (v): to increase in extent, volume, number, amount, intensity, or scope

In some companies, escalation is a "dirty word"—if two people disagree, they have to keep the disagreement to themselves and may never resolve it. In other companies, escalations of minor issues happen so often that managers can't get their work done.

Escalation is *not* a "dirty word." It's a manager's job to clear obstacles (including disagreements) that prevent his/her direct reports from getting their work done. On the other hand, escalations should not be over-used. If people are clear about their roles and decision authorities within the context of their manager's role and objectives, they should be able to resolve many of their own disagreements. The following is an effective process:

- If two members of the same team disagree, each asks themselves the question "If our manager were here *right now*, what would he/she have us do?"

- If the members still cannot agree, they may ask for support from an independent third party (for example, someone in HR or an outside consultant).

- If the previous two options fail to gain agreement, *both members simultaneously approach their manager*, explain the situation without blaming, and ask for guidance.

If the two people are on different teams, the process is the same except that each approaches his/her own manager at the same time. Those two managers may then need to get together to resolve the issue—and may even need to call on their own manager if their best efforts at resolution are unsuccessful.

The accountability-based escalation process

What would our manager want? ⟶ Agree ☺ / Disagree ☹ ► Let's ask an independent third party for advice ⟶ Agree ☺ / Disagree ☹ ► Let's go together and talk to our manager

In an accountability-based company...

- Managers understand they are accountable to remove barriers that prevent their direct reports from working effectively.

- Employees make their best efforts to resolve disagreements with the overall good of the team, department, or company in mind.

- People recognize that disagreements are about the work—they are not personal.

- Employees can escalate to their managers in a timely way and without fear of reprisal if their best efforts to resolve a disagreement have failed.

"Honest disagreement is often a good sign of progress." (Mahatma Gandhi, Indian political and spiritual leader, 1869–1948)

F is for felt-fair pay

Feel (v):   to undergo passive experience of; to have one's sensibilities markedly affected by; to be aware of by instinct or inference

Fair (adj):   pleasing to the eye or mind; marked by impartiality and honesty; free from self-interest, prejudice, or favouritism; conforming with the established rules; sufficient but not ample

Pay (n):   something paid for a purpose and especially as a salary or wage

Most people want to be paid fairly for the work they do, and to feel others within their organization are also paid fairly. The best way to promote fairness is for a company to have pay bands that match the levels of work complexity—in other words, pay is based on the complexity of work in a role as opposed to the individual who is doing the work. And as long as the individual fits the role well in terms of having the right information processing capability (see page 39), possessing appropriate knowledge and skills, and valuing the work, the pay will be seen as fair.

Although some organizations try to place people in pay bands through an "objective" points system, the level of pay for a role is, in fact, a judgment that a role's manager and manager-once-removed make. The final decision on pay must be made in the context of discussions with other managers/managers-once-removed and HR representatives, and within a company's established compensation system.

In an accountability-based company...

- Pay bands line up with the organization's levels of work complexity.

- People feel fairly paid for the work they do.

- Managers recommend pay levels for their direct reports.

- Managers-once-removed meet with their own direct reports to discuss the effects of pay changes for employees-once-removed within the three-tier unit (see page 88).

- Managers-once-removed work with their direct reports, supported by HR, to agree on fair and equitable pay for their employees-once-removed within broad company compensation guidelines.

- There is openness about pay bands and about reasons for anomalies.

- People understand that pay takes into account skill scarcity and other temporary market conditions, but the environment is constantly under review and adjustments made as things change.

"It is not wealth one asks for, but just enough to preserve one's dignity, to work unhampered, to be generous, frank, and independent." (W. Somerset Maugham, English dramatist and novelist, 1874–1965)

F is also for form follows function

Form (n):   the shape and structure of something as distinguished from
                  its material

Function (n):   the action for which a person or thing is specially fitted or
                  used, or for which a thing exists

A company's structure needs to be designed so the company can most effectively achieve its strategy. This involves having the right number of layers of management, and the right types of work taking place in the right groups. Failure to pay attention to how work is grouped and layered wastes effort, time, and money.

In an accountability-based company...

- There are exactly the right number of management layers, with effective distribution of accountability and authority.

- Work is grouped to minimize cross-boundary friction and coordination costs.

- If the strategy (the function) changes, senior managers automatically review the organization's structure (the form).

"The structures that we create and use must match their intended purpose—no more and no less—to be the most effective." (David Allen, American management consultant, trainer, and author, 1945–)

G is for gap

Gap (n):   a separation in space; an incomplete or deficient area

Whatever a role's level of work complexity (see page 52), the role holder's manager should be capable of, and working at, one level higher. If a manager is working more than one level above, it causes a gap. Someone who is in a gap with his/her manager might say,

> "My manager appears to have his head in the clouds and doesn't appreciate the issues I have to deal with in my work."

> "I often have to do my manager's job, and it's a real struggle—I don't think I do it very well."

> "My manager seems to think I'm really dumb."

while the manager in a gap situation might say,

> "I have to spend an inordinate amount of time explaining things to my direct report, who still doesn't understand the needs well enough."

> "I feel like I'm always being pulled down into the weeds rather than concentrating on what really matters."

In an accountability-based company...

- Each employee has a manager capable of doing, and performing, work that is one level higher in complexity.

- Gaps are not built into the structure (except perhaps temporarily during a transition period, with careful thought and awareness of how to manage the gap).

Note: It can be OK for an individual contributor to be in a gap situation with his/her manager, particularly if the role provides direct output support to that manager (see *Output*, page 62 and *Individual contributors*, page 38).

"Every one of us gets through the tough times because somebody is there, standing in the gap to close it for us." (Oprah Winfrey, American actress and television talk show host, 1954–)

G is also for goals

Goal (n):   the end toward which effort is directed

We need goals if we are not to wander aimlessly through work and life. In an organization, people need to understand what the strategy is and how their work fits into that strategy. People are usually more effective if they know *why* they are doing things—how achieving their goals helps their manager achieve his/hers, and so on right up to the top layers of the company.

Although managers determine their direct reports' overall goals, managers and direct reports should work together to flesh out the details of how the goals will be achieved, and with what resources. Managers also need to make sure that the overall goals fit within the timespan of a direct report's level of work (see *Level of work complexity,* page 52).

There are various other terms for a goal—objectives, key performance indicators (KPIs), key results areas (KRAs).... The terminology is less important than ensuring people are set up for success by matching goals to the level of work complexity in a role.

In other words...

For this level	The longest goal is
1	3 months
2	1 year
3	2 years
4	5 years
5	10 years

In an accountability-based company...

- All employees understand the company's strategy.

- All employees have clearly defined goals with timespans that are appropriate for their role.

- Everyone understands how his/her own goals help the company achieve its strategy.

- People are evaluated not just on whether or not they achieved their goals, but under what conditions and how they did it.

"Without goals and plans to reach them, you are like a ship that has set sail with no destination." (Fitzhugh Dodson, American psychologist and author, 1923–1993)

H is for hierarchy

Hierarchy (n):   a division of angels; the classification of a group of people according to ability or to economic, social, or professional standing

Many people work in a hierarchical organization. To some, the word hierarchy denotes bureaucracy and power—things that stifle creativity and initiative. However, an accountability-based hierarchy is not about power. Instead, it's a way of grouping roles according to their level of work complexity, thus ensuring

- the right people are doing the work the company needs to get done,

- people have clear roles and appropriate authority to act, and

- each managerial layer adds value.

In an accountability-based company...

- There are just the right number of layers of management—not too many, not too few.

- People know who is accountable for the work they do, and who to go to when they have problems.

- People know what their own work is, and what their boundaries are.

"Every seeming equality conceals a hierarchy." (Mason Cooley, American aphorist, 1927–2002)

I is for individual contributors

Individual (n): a particular being or thing as distinguished from a class, species, or collection. (Obsolete meaning: inseparable)

Contributor (n): one who gives or supplies in common with others; one who plays a significant part in bringing about an end or result

Individual contributors are people who provide specialized knowledge or skills, such as a legal advisor or IT expert. They usually don't have direct reports, but this doesn't mean they perform only level 1 work (see *Level of work complexity*, page 52). An individual contributor can work at any level in an organization, and can do work that supports roles up to two levels above or below that of his/her own.

In an accountability-based company...

- Individual contributors are recognized and valued for the work they do.

- Individual contributors are not required to manage people to obtain pay or status increases.

"To a specialist, his specialty is the whole of everything and if his specialty is in good order, and it generally is, then everything must be succeeding." (Gertrude Stein, American author, 1874–1946)

I is also for information processing capability

Information (n):   the communication or reception of knowledge or intelligence

Process (v):   to subject to examination or analysis

Work involves thinking (see *Work*, page 100), and whenever people work they are processing information to make decisions. As work becomes more complex, there are more pieces of information to consider, and more chance that changing one thing could affect many others. How an individual processes information indicates what level of work he/she is most suited for. For example, a person who is most happy making straight choices within guidelines is probably best suited to level 1 work (see *Level of work complexity*, page 52), while a person who likes to explore multiple avenues and consider "well, if I did this, then that might happen and on the other hand if I did this then that might happen..." is likely best suited to level 3 work. Matching information processing capability to role complexity is important to ensure the work can get done effectively and the role holder is being set up for success.

Information processing capability is not something people can improve through training. Everyone develops at his/her own speed to a maximum level that is different for each person. (See also *Capability*, page 8 and *Role-person fit*, page 78.)

In an accountability-based company...

- People have the right information processing capability for the work they need to do.

- Managers' information processing capability is one level higher than that of their direct reports.

- MoRs make effective judgments about when EoRs will be capable of working at the next level up.

"Thinking is the hardest work there is, which is why so few managers engage in it." (Henry Ford, American automobile industrialist, 1863–1947)

And I is for interdependence

Interdependent (adj): mutually dependent

Dependent (adj): determined or conditioned by another; relying on another for support

In most companies, groups and role holders depend on each other's outputs to meet their own business goals (see also *Cross-boundary relationships,* page 104). When designing an organization structure, it's important to understand where interdependencies exist and how best to manage interdependent groups. There are three different degrees of interdependence[2]:

Pooled
    There is little interaction between groups, but all groups must work effectively to meet overall business goals. (Such groups do not need to be under a common manager.)

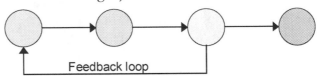

Sequential
    There is a handoff from one group to the next, where the work outputs of the first group become the inputs of the next. (Such groups may or may not be under a common manager.)

Reciprocal
    The work outputs of one group immediately affect the other group, and vice versa. Each unit's work is contingent on the work of the other, requiring constant mutual adjustment. (Such groups should be organized under a common manager as low as possible in the organization hierarchy.)

---

[2] As defined by James D. Thompson in his book *Organizations in Action,* New York: McGraw Hill, 1967

Grouping highly (reciprocally) interdependent processes or groups under a common manager reduces the need for coordinating activities and processes such as committees and cross-functional teams, and allows escalated problems to be dealt with promptly.

In an accountability-based company...

- Work is grouped appropriately to minimize cross-functional friction and promote goal achievement.

- Different groups understand how each contributes to the other, and why it's necessary to work collaboratively.

- If problems arise, people understand who they need to talk to and can determine when escalation is required.

"It is a good thing to be dependent on each other for something: it makes us civil and peaceable." (Sojourner Truth, American Abolitionist and women's rights activist, c.1797–1883)

J is for jam-up

Jam (v):   to become blocked or wedged; to become unworkable through the jamming of a movable part; to make unintelligible by sending out interfering signals or messages

If someone is performing work at the same level of complexity as his/her manager, they are both probably experiencing a jam-up (also known as *compression*). A direct report in a jam-up with his/her manager might say,

> "My manager is always interfering and won't leave me alone to get on with my work."

> "My manager doesn't set appropriate context for my work—I usually go elsewhere for this."

> "My manager and I work more like colleagues than roles in a reporting relationship."

> "My manager and I both do the same things, so work gets duplicated."

And a manager experiencing a jam-up with his/her direct reports might say,

> "I share my work with my employees as equal partners. It helps keep them motivated, although it does make my job less challenging."

> "There's a lot of work I could delegate but I don't, because I don't want my direct reports to get all the interesting stuff even though they keep asking for it."

In an accountability-based company...

- Each employee has a manager capable of doing, and performing, work that is one level higher in complexity.

- Managers don't interfere with or duplicate their direct reports' work.

- Jam-ups are not built into the structure (except perhaps temporarily, with careful thought and awareness of how to manage the jam-up).

Note: It can be OK for an individual contributor (a role with no direct reports who provides specialized knowledge or skills) to be operating at the same level of work complexity as his/her manager.

"The best executive is the one who has sense enough to pick good men to do what he wants done, and the self-restraint to keep from meddling with them while they do it." (Theodore Roosevelt, 26th US President, 1858–1919)

J is also for Jaques

Elliott Jaques (1917–2003) developed and refined the *requisite organization* management model during a period of over fifty years of research. The work began in 1948 when Wilfred (later Lord) Brown, CEO of Glacier Metal, engaged Jaques to research as scientifically as possible the fundamental properties of his organization. Brown wanted to know what enabled work to be carried out effectively, efficiently, and with trust and fairness for all involved. The 17-year research project led Jaques to determine the following foundational elements of requisite organization (accountability-based management), which he continued to explore and refine up to his death:

- A clear and unapologetic hierarchy, with exactly the right number of layers, where each person has only one manager.

- Clear accountability, with managers held accountable for their direct reports' outputs, and each person knowing to whom they are accountable, for what, by when.

- People in roles that match their current capability, and a process for mapping talent to future roles.

- People able to exercise an appropriate level of discretion and creativity within their roles.

- Trust based on clear expectations, consistent behaviours, and fair and equitable treatment of employees.

Jaques was born in Toronto, Ontario, educated at the University of Toronto, and studied medicine at Johns Hopkins University before receiving his Ph.D in social relations from Harvard University. During World War II he moved to England, where he remained after the war, studying under German psychoanalyst Melanie Klein. He was a founding member, in 1946, of the Tavistock Institute of Human Relations. If you want to read in more detail about his work, the following are available:

Requisite Organization, A Total System for Effective Managerial Organization and Managerial Leadership for the 21st Century (Baltimore: Cason Hall & Co. Publishers, 2006); ISBN 1-886436-04-5; Hardcover, 336 pages Revised edition, 2006, Cason Hall & Co. Publishers Ltd.

Executive Leadership: A Practical Guide to Managing Complexity
Elliott Jaques, Stephen D. Clement, Ronnie Lessem (Foreword by)
ISBN 0-9621070-1-8; Hardcover, 317 pages
Second Printing, 1994, Cason Hall & Co. Publishers Ltd.

Executive Leadership: A Practical Guide to Managing Complexity
Elliott Jaques, Stephen D. Clement, Ronnie Lessem (Foreword by)
ISBN: 978-0-631-19313-5; Paperback, 344 pages
April 1994, Wiley-Blackwell

Human Capability, A Study of Human Capability and its Application
Elliott Jaques, Kathryn Cason
ISBN 0-9621070-7-7; Hardcover, 165 pages
1994, Cason Hall & Co. Publishers Ltd.

Further information and resources are also available at the Requisite Organization International Institute website (www.requisite.org) and at the Global Organization Design Society (GO) website (www.globalro.org).

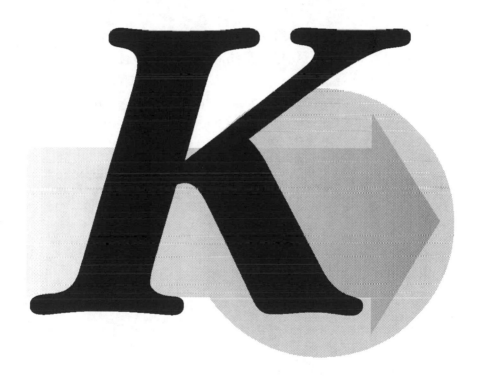

K is for knowledge

Knowledge (n):   the fact or condition of knowing something with familiarity gained through experience or association

To do a job well, you need appropriate knowledge, which is something you gain from education and experience. While a manager ensures his/her direct reports receive appropriate coaching to do their current work, a manager-once-removed ensures employees two levels down get opportunities to gain knowledge for career development.

In an accountability-based company...

- Managers are aware of what coaching their direct reports need, and see that they get it.

- Managers-once-removed work with their employees-once-removed to develop career plans, and provide opportunities to help employees-once-removed achieve their goals.

"It is possible to fly without motors, but not without knowledge and skill."
(Wilbur Wright, American airplane designer and aviation pioneer, 1867–1912)

L is for level of work complexity

Level (n): a position in a scale

Work (n): activity in which one exerts strength or faculties to do or perform something; sustained physical or mental effort to overcome obstacles and achieve an objective or result

Complex (adj): composed of two or more parts

In every company there is work to be done. Some of it is complex, some of it is simple, and all of it is important. The principle of level of work complexity (LW) is based on research done over many years by Elliott Jaques (1917-2003) and described in his book *Requisite Organization*. Jaques found that the way to establish the level of work complexity in a role was through the longest task assigned to that role (the role's *timespan of discretion*, see page 89*). His theory was that the longer a manager gave a role holder to do a certain task, the more other things that person had to juggle and balance to get everything done at the right time, and therefore the more complex the role's work. In his research, he found that the timespans of discretion tended to group into a maximum of seven layers, or strata.

Not all organizations have seven layers of work complexity. A small family-owned business might have two. A medium-sized business or a profit-and-loss unit of a larger organization usually has five. Most world-wide corporations have seven. In his later life, Jaques identified some super-corporations with eight levels of work complexity.

The following diagram gives an example of the type of work and longest task timespans for the seven levels of work complexity.

	LW7 Purpose/Philosophy	Manage an enterprise
20 y	**LW6** Global Opportunities	Manage businesses
10 y	**LW5** New Business Models	Manage a business
5 y	**LW4** New Products/Services/Processes	Manage a function
2 y	**LW3** Processes/Systems	Manage managers
1 y	**LW2** Continuous Improvement	Manage a team
3 mo	**LW1** Customer Service/Quality	Manage self

Notes:

- Although timespan of longest task is the only objective way to measure work complexity, there are other indicators, such as having a larger number of variables or unknowns to deal with.

- Whether or not you have direct reports does not determine level of work complexity. Individual contributors could be at any level in an organization, and there are some companies where front-line work is level 2.

In an accountability-based company...

- People understand how many levels of work are required to achieve the company's strategy.

- Managers assign task as a clear "what by when" so the complexity of work in a role is clearly defined and understood.

- Each level is staffed with people capable of working at that level.

- Each role holder has a manager capable of working at the next level up.

- Each level of work is valued.

"There are no menial jobs, only menial attitudes." (William Bennett, American federal official and author, 1943–)

M is for manager

Manager (n):   a person who conducts business or household affairs; a person whose work or profession is management; a person who directs a team or athlete

Management (n):   the conducting or supervising of something (as a business)

Managers meet their goals through a combination of their own work and that of their direct reports. They are accountable for their own personal effectiveness, for the outputs of their direct reports, for building and sustaining an effective team, and for carrying out the following managerial leadership practices:

- Holding regular team meetings.
- Setting context for direct reports' work.
- Planning their own and their department's work.
- Assigning work clearly.
- Appraising direct reports' personal effectiveness.
- Carrying out merit reviews.
- Providing coaching for direct reports.
- Continually improving processes.
- Selecting and inducting team members.
- Initiating removal from role (not necessarily from the company) for individuals who are not suited to their role.

In an accountability-based company...

- Each employee has a manager capable of doing work that is one level higher in complexity.
- Managers are held to account for whether or not their direct reports achieve their goals and required results, and for how they did their work.
- Managers carry out their managerial leadership practices, and are evaluated on how well they do so.
- There are consequences for managers who don't perform their managerial leadership practices effectively.

"You do not lead by hitting people over the head—that's assault, not leadership."
(Dwight G. Eisenhower, US General, 1890–1969)

56

M is also for manager-once-removed

Removed (adj):   distant in degree of relationship

Your manager-once-removed
(MoR) is your manager's
manager—sometimes called a
skip-level manager—and you are
that person's employee-once-
removed (EoR). If you have
direct reports who manage
people, you are the manager-

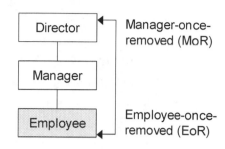

once-removed to those people, and they are your employees-once-
removed. An MoR's accountabilities differ from those of a manager
(see page 3). It is the MoR's job to manage the talent pool, ensure
EoRs are paid fairly and equitably, provide mentoring to EoRs, and
ensure there are successors for key roles. MoRs must also make sure
their own direct reports are effective managers.

Groups of MoRs need to meet at least once a year to discuss their
EoRs' level of work and pay bands, and identify development
opportunities for EoRs.

If you are an MoR, this means you have to know all your EoRs—at
least visually, and preferably by name. You will need to know who
they are, where they work, their important career aspirations, how
they're doing, and their potential for promotion. Your direct reports
(your EoRs' managers) can help you with this. You don't have to
meet with each of your EoRs once a week, but you should be
meeting with the high-potential ones regularly enough that they know
their careers are being considered. Further, your EoRs can provide
valuable feedback on how your direct reports are doing as managers.
MoRs also need to be approachable and available to any EoRs who
want career development advice, mentoring, or to discuss a situation
where they feel their manager hasn't treated them fairly.

On the other side, if you want some career guidance but your MoR
doesn't seem to know you exist, let your manager know and ask for
help in approaching your MoR to let him or her know your hopes
and expectations... don't wait to be sought out.

And yes, if you are a CEO or President, you have MoR accountabilities too!

In an accountability-based company…

- MoRs do the following:
  - make sure their direct reports exercise the managerial leadership practices listed on page 56.
  - establish EoR work levels and placement in compensation bands.
  - develop the talent pool of EoRs (includes mentoring and career planning).
  - assess EoRs' current and future potential capability (see *Capability*, page 8).
  - plan succession for roles one level down.
  - ensure EoRs are treated fairly and equitably across the organization.
  - finalize EoRs' placement in/removal from role and, when appropriate, removal from the organization.
  - ensure EoR's cross-boundary relationships are defined and effective.
- Employees feel comfortable going to their MoR for career planning.
- Employees can approach their MoR, without fear of retribution, if they have a problem with their manager that best efforts have failed to resolve.

"The world is so empty if one thinks only of mountains, rivers, and cities, but to know that there is someone who, though distant, thinks and feels with us—this makes the earth for us an inhabited garden." (Johann Wolfgang von Goethe, German dramatist, novelist, poet, and scientist, 1749–1832)

N is for no surprises, no excuses

Surprise (v):   to take unawares; to strike with wonder or amazement especially because unexpected

Excuse (n):   an expression of regret for failure to do something

The "early warning system" is a cornerstone of accountability-based management. It means that direct reports keep their manager appropriately informed about the progress of tasks, and let their manager know immediately if they sense they will meet their goal *either ahead of or behind* the scheduled time, or if resources will be consumed *at a greater or lesser rate* than planned. Early warning allows managers to consider other things that will be affected by this change, inform their own manager, and modify their plans accordingly. But this doesn't mean managers need to be breathing down their direct reports' necks as they do their work. It does mean managers need to set up the right processes and environment so their direct reports feel comfortable telling them how things are going.

In an accountability-based company...

- Managers know how direct reports are progressing with their work without it feeling like constant supervision.

- There is no blame attached to not meeting a goal, as long as your manager finds out about it early enough to make alternative plans.

- "I didn't know" is not an acceptable excuse for a manager to give.

- There's no such thing as good news or bad news. It's just news.

"It is wise to direct your anger towards problems—not people; to focus your energies on answers—not excuses." (William Arthur Ward, American, author, pastor, and teacher, 1921–1994)

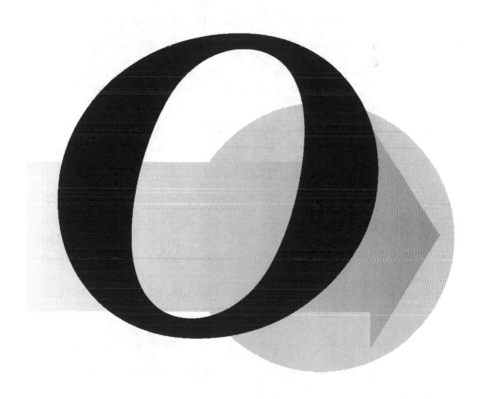

O is for output

Output (n):   mental or artistic production; the amount produced by a person in a given time

An output is something you produce. It can be something concrete, like a departmental budget, or something abstract like customer service. Under accountability-based principles, there are five types of output:

1. Direct output (DO)—you produce it yourself.

2. Aided direct output (ADO)—someone helps you produce it.

3. Direct output support (DOS)—you help someone produce it.

4. Delegated direct output (DDO)— you ask a direct report to produce it (see *QQTR* on page 70), but you're still accountable for the results.

5. Policy controlled direct output (PCDO)—you produce it yourself, but have to get approval—e.g. from Legal or Communications—before you send it out anywhere.

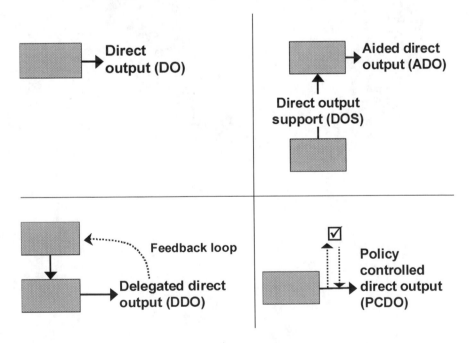

For most people this is just an interesting (or not) snippet of information. It's useful when designing an organization because it helps identify who is truly accountable for what work, which roles need to be grouped together, and who needs to have the authority to ask for what across boundaries. (Also see *Cross-boundary role relationships*, page 104).

In an accountability-based company...

- People know what work is their own direct output and what they delegate.

- Managers accept full accountability for work they've delegated.

- Work is grouped appropriately to facilitate aided direct output and direct output support.

- People understand when sign off is required on their direct outputs, and where to go for that approval.

"Nothing can be produced out of nothing." (Diogenes Laertius, 3rd century Greek writer)

P is for performance

Performance (n):   the execution of an action; the fulfillment of a claim, promise, or request

Surveys indicate that one of the most important elements of job satisfaction is for people to understand the performance measurement system and how they're doing. This requires more than an annual performance review: frequent and timely feedback on how people are performing ensures they stay on track and surfaces problems early. It doesn't need to be a lengthy one-on-one meeting: managers can recognize good performance (or the lack of it) with an informal verbal comment.

Performance is not just about producing required outputs within the expected timeframe. Managers need to consider how people achieved their results (their effectiveness) and under what conditions. For example, someone who achieved only 60% of plan because of unexpected market conditions over which he/she had no control might have performed better during the year than someone who achieved 110% of plan because some business was handed to him/her on a plate.

Performance measurement is not a purely objective exercise, nor can it be made to be so. It's a manager's judgment, and a manager's work involves making this type of judgment. If a manager consistently makes poor judgments about direct reports, that's an issue for the MoR!

In an accountability-based company...

- People understand and value the performance management system.

- Managers provide frequent and timely feedback to their direct reports, then provide coaching to make up any shortfalls.

- Performance evaluation is based not just on what is achieved, but on how and under what conditions.

- Employees can appeal to their MoR, without fear of retribution, if they feel unfairly evaluated.

"People forget how fast you did a job—but they remember how well you did it."
(Howard Newton, American advertising executive, 1903–1951)

P is also for personal effectiveness

Effective (n):   producing a decided, decisive, or desired effect; readiness for service or action

Personal (adj):   of, relating to, or affecting a person; done in person without the intervention of another

Personal effectiveness is how well someone applies him/herself to the tasks in a role. When evaluating a direct report's personal effectiveness, a manager considers the results that have been achieved, how well the person has applied his or her capability, skills, and knowledge, and what behaviours the person has exhibited in carrying out the work. The manager does not make these judgments in isolation—the manager-once-removed ensures fairness and equity by being aware of and comparing the judgments made by his or her own direct reports.

Judging a person's effectiveness in role, involves answering the following questions:

Does this person seem suited for the role?

In other words, does the person's current applied capability (see page 8) match the role's level of work complexity (see page 52)?

If **no** then,	If **yes**, then
• Is this person's effectiveness above what is required for the role? or • Is this person's effectiveness below what is required for the role?	• Does this person work like somebody in the top half, the bottom half, or right in the middle of what you expect? • If in the top half, does it seem like this person is getting ready to move ahead to the next level?

In an accountability-based company…

- Everyone can be counted on to use their best efforts at work.

- Personal effectiveness is not measured by complicated points scales: it's a manager's judgment.

- Personal effectiveness is not just about achieving results: it's about *how* people achieve results.

- Managers-once-removed meet with their own direct reports to discuss the performance of employees-once-removed within the three-tier unit (see page 88), and compare the judgments to ensure fairness and equity.

"An empowered organization is one in which individuals have the knowledge, skill, desire, and opportunity to personally succeed in a way that leads to collective organizational success." (Stephen R. Covey, American author and consultant, 1932–)

Q is for QQTR

Quantity (n):	an indefinite amount or number; a determinate or estimated amount
Quality (n):	peculiar and essential character
Time (n):	the measured or measurable period during which an action, process, or condition exists or continues
Resources (n):	a source of supply or support; an available means

QQTRs are the elements of a task—the "what by when, and with what." When a manager asks a direct report to do something, it's important for the manager to set context as to why the work needs to be done, and for both the manager and the direct report to understand these elements:

Quantity	How much, how many
Quality	How well it should be done, and any special criteria or conditions to be met (including avoiding any undesired results)
Time	When it needs to be completed
Resources	What people, money, authorities are available

Most managers don't assign work clearly. They usually know when and how they want things to be done, but often forget to be specific. As many direct reports feel they shouldn't ask too many questions, just get the job done, it's not surprising that they don't always meet their manager's expectations. If you're a manager, be aware of the QQTR elements and make them as specific as possible when delegating work.

When your manager assigns a task using QQTR, you need to consider if it's feasible or not. If it's feasible, be clear that you accept the task. If not, let your manager know immediately so the two of you can negotiate (see *Commitments* on page 12). For example,

Sue :	Bob, I'd like you analyze our customer satisfaction survey results and give me a graph showing the change from last year.
Bob:	When do you want this to be done?
Sue:	By next Monday.
Bob:	I can do it by next Monday, but the monthly budget won't get done as well. Which would you prefer?

Sue: I need both. What if I ask Sunil to help you with the budget?

Bob: Yes, that will work. I can do it by Monday.

Remember that if, while a task is being carried out, any one of the QQTR elements changes, it affects the others. Use the early warning system: let your manager know immediately so you can renegotiate and your manager can plan accordingly.

In an accountability-based company...

- Managers always make sure direct reports understand the context and purpose of any delegated work.

- Managers always make sure their direct reports understand the QQTRs of delegated work.

- People feel comfortable questioning and negotiating QQTRs with their manager.

- Managers and direct reports renegotiate QQTRs when situations change.

"Quality is never an accident; it is always the result of intelligent effort."
(John Ruskin, English critic, essayist, and reformer, 1819–1900)

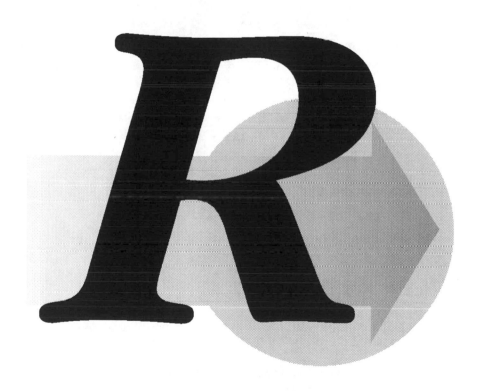

R is for responsibility

Responsible (adj):   able to choose for oneself between right and wrong

Accountability and responsibility are not the same thing: accountability is the obligation to answer for an action, while responsibility is a felt obligation to act within the values of an organization. For example, if a customer complains to someone who is not accountable for handling complaints, the responsible thing for that person to do is see that the complaint goes to the right place for resolution. It may be true, but is not helpful, to say "Sorry, that's not my job."

People often take on work to help out their colleagues, or because they see it needs to be done and no-one else is doing it. These are noble reasons, and providing short-term help to colleagues is not a problem if you have the time. But taking on more permanent work because you feel responsible for it—as opposed to because you are accountable for it—can lead to overload and duplication at the expense of meeting your own performance goals. The best thing is to alert your manager to the fact that you feel responsible for this work and clarify which role is best suited to take it on.

In an accountability-based company...

- Employees feel a shared sense of responsibility to make the company the best it can be.

- Employees can differentiate between responsibly helping someone and being fully accountable for something.

- People don't automatically assume other role holders' accountabilities.

- Employees ensure that, whatever actions they take, they do not intentionally harm any other employees.

"I believe that every right implies a responsibility; every opportunity an obligation; every possession a duty." (John D. Rockefeller, Jr., American philanthropist, 1874–1960)

R is also for rewards and recognition

Reward (n): something that is given in return for good or evil done or received and especially that is offered or given for some service or attainment

Recognition (n): special notice or attention

People need to know how well they're doing, and they appreciate recognition for doing a good job. Compensation is one way to recognize people, but recognition over and above compensation lets people know their contribution is truly appreciated and inspires people to do their best.

It is a manager's job to provide rewards and recognition. Unfortunately, many managers simply expect excellent work and forget to let people know when they are meeting these expectations. Instead, they tend to focus on what goes wrong or praise only truly exceptional work.

Recognition doesn't have to be in the form of bonuses or other cash rewards. Something as simple as a "thank you" e-mail from the CEO to someone further down in the organization might be all that's needed when someone has done an excellent job. When developing a rewards and recognition program, managers need to work with employees to find out what they really value as a reward and appreciate as recognition.

In an accountability-based company...

- Managers ensure people feel appreciated for doing good work.

- Employees receive regular feedback on how they are doing.

- Rewards and recognition are in a form that employees truly value.

- Managers have sufficient authority to provide appropriate rewards.

"In the arena of human life the honours and rewards fall to those who show their good qualities in action." (Aristotle, Greek philosopher, scientist, and physician, 384–322 BC)

And R is for role clarity

Role: A character assigned or assumed; a socially expected behaviour pattern usually determined by an individual's status in a particular society

Very often, when people are interviewed about what they most want in their roles, they express a need for role clarity. A lack of role clarity leads to increased stress, duplication, and unnecessary escalations. There are four aspects of role clarity—and all need to be aligned if the role is to be carried out effectively:

- How the role holder perceives the role.

- How the role holder's manager perceives the role.

- How others in the organization perceive the role.

- How the role is actually carried out.

Getting role clarity is not difficult, but is often neglected. It involves having conversations with all concerned to ensure everyone has the same understanding, and then putting mechanisms in place to ensure people are acting out their roles as described:

- The role's manager writes a high-level description of the role— the overall purpose and perhaps an outline of the accountabilities— and shares this with his/her own manager (the role's manager-once-removed) for approval.

- Once the manager and manager-once-removed are in agreement, the manager shares the draft role description with the role holder and asks him/her to add more information.

- The role holder adds more detail such as what's included, what's excluded, major accountabilities, decision-making rights, and any cross-boundary authorities—and shares this with his/her manager.

- The whole team (manager and all direct reports) share their role descriptions and discuss to ensure everyone on the same team understands each other's role, that the work is at the right level and linked appropriately to the manager's work, and that there are no overlaps or gaps. The manager-once-removed gives final approval.

- Role holders share their role descriptions with others outside the team as necessary to gain understanding and clarify cross-boundary role relationships (see *Cross-boundary relationships* on page 104).

- The role descriptions are kept current (ideally posted on a shared network that everyone in the company can access) and are used for regular performance feedback discussions.

In an accountability-based company…

- Role descriptions reflect the role's level of work complexity.

- People know who does what and can direct enquiries accordingly.

- People know who has authority to make what decisions.

- Managers and direct reports review role descriptions regularly and make adjustments as necessary.

- Performance evaluation systems are linked to the accountabilities outlined on role descriptions.

"No law or ordinance is mightier than understanding." (Plato, Greek author and philosopher, 427–347 BC)

And R is for role-person fit

Role (n):   a character assigned or assumed

Fit (v):   to be suitable for or to harmonize with

Role-person fit is how well a person's information processing capability (see page 39), knowledge and skills, valuing of the work, and behaviour match what is required in a role:

How well a person fits a role is a function of

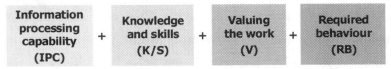

Information processing capability (IPC) + Knowledge and skills (K/S) + Valuing the work (V) + Required behaviour (RB)

Of these only information processing capability (IPC), which is inherent and develops with time, cannot be improved through training and coaching. Because someone with a lower level of IPC than is required by a role is almost guaranteed to fail, managers and managers-once-removed need to work together to ensure they select people with the right information processing capability for particular roles.

There are some people who will never value a particular type of work and are therefore not a good fit for a role—for example, a highly skilled technical individual contributor who does not have any interest in managing people should not be placed in a managerial role "because that's the only way we can pay you what you're worth." In most cases, however, people can work with their manager to develop knowledge and skills, to learn how to value the work, and to understand how to demonstrate required behaviour (behaviour that is in line with company values).

If someone who is over-qualified is placed in a role, he or she may start to invent work that better matches his/her IPC and skills/knowledge. It may be useful work, or it may be perceived as mischief. The person will likely also feel underpaid. It's important for managers to address the issue of role-person fit, and not to artificially inflate the role's pay or boundaries to accommodate an over-qualified candidate.

Sometimes people take roles for which they are over-qualified (have greater IPC than is required) because they do something else outside of work where they use their full capability—for example, volunteer work or supporting a spouse's business—and do not want additional challenge. This is workable, as long as the person, the manager, and the manager-once-removed are aware of the situation, are clear that the role expectations must still be met, and do not allow the role (or the pay) to grow to match the person's capability.

In an accountability-based company…

- People have the right information processing capability, knowledge, and skills to perform effectively in their role.

- People value their own and others' work, and are not required to do work they don't value just so they can be paid fairly.

- People demonstrate appropriate behaviour in their role.

- People are given sufficient opportunities to develop role-related skills and knowledge.

- Employees can appeal to their manager-once-removed if their manager does not demonstrate appropriate managerial behaviour.

"Anyone who is capable of getting themselves made President should on no account be allowed to do the job." (Douglas Adams, English humorist and science fiction novelist, 1952–2001)

S is for service providing and receiving

Service (n):   contribution to the welfare of others

Within any organization there are usually people who need to get a service from others who work for a different manager. For example, Human Resources provides services in the form of help with recruitment and hiring to people across an organization; Information Technology provides hardware, software, and consulting services. If technology is outsourced, an outside company provides these services, although someone within the company must still be accountable for the quality of the services provided. Service providing and receiving is the most widespread form of cross-boundary relationship (see *Cross-boundary relationships*, page 104). People can run into problems if it is not clear who has what authority and what obligations each party has to the other, and if commitments are not made and managed effectively (see page 12).

If the service provider and the service receiver are in the same organization, it should be easy for the two parties to meet and agree on required service levels and authorities. In case of disagreement, the respective managers and managers-once-removed can help clarify what's needed. If a service is outsourced, however, there is less control and potentially poorer understanding. It's harder work, but still possible for those involved to be very clear about their expectations and what the roles and authorities are. Often a formal Service Level Agreement can specify what's required on both sides.

In an accountability-based company…

- Work is grouped appropriately to minimize cross-functional friction.

- Role holders, their managers, and their managers-once-removed work together to define and approve cross-boundary relationships.

- Service receivers and service providers meet regularly to clarify needs and expectations.

- Service receivers and service providers manage their commitments impeccably and escalate in a timely way to their respective managers if they cannot resolve a problem themselves.

- When asking for a service, service receivers clearly describe their expectations and the reasons behind them.

- Service providers

  - understand what they must provide, by when, to what quality, and why.

  - advise service receivers in plenty of time if they are unable to meet their commitments.

- If work is outsourced, a full-time company employee is still held accountable for the quality, quantity, and timeliness of that outsourced work.

"The service you do for others is the rent you pay for the time you spend on earth." (Mohammed Ali, Macedonian governor and later viceroy of Egypt, c.1769–1849)

S is also for skills

Skill (n):   the ability to use one's knowledge effectively and readily in execution or performance; dexterity or coordination especially in the execution of learned physical tasks; a learned power of doing something competently; a developed aptitude or ability

Along with knowledge, skills are an element of the role-person fit formula (a person's suitability for a particular role—see page 78). If a role candidate (or incumbent) is lacking in skills, it is relatively easy to resolve the issue with coaching, training, or work experience. Managers need to be watching for skill deficiencies, coaching where appropriate, and ensuring appropriate training is provided.

In an accountability-based company...

- People have, or can easily obtain, the skills they need to meet their accountabilities.

- Managers are aware of skill gaps and take actions to close them.

- People are comfortable requesting training if they feel they need it.

"A smooth sea never made a skilled mariner." (English proverb)

And S is for span of control

Span (n):   an extent, stretch, reach, or spread between two limits

Control (n):   power or authority to guide or manage

Span of control is the number of direct reports a manager has. A more appropriate term might be "span of support," as it really relates to how a manager can best support his/her team members. A manager with too many direct reports cannot provide adequate coaching, recognition, and feedback to team members. A manager with too few direct reports will tend to "dip down" and do extra work that distracts him or her from important managerial work.

There is no precise number that represents the "right" span of control, but there are principles to help establish what is best for a particular role. The manager must be able to

- effectively judge the personal effectiveness of each direct report.

- provide the required coaching and performance feedback to each direct report.

- effectively perform his/her own work.

The following factors affect the size of a manager's span of control:

- The similarity of direct reports' work
  (more similar = more direct reports possible).

- The complexity of direct reports' work
  (more complex = fewer direct reports possible).

- Direct reports' geographic location
  (more widespread = fewer direct reports possible).

- Direct reports' capability, knowledge, and skills
  (greater levels = more direct reports possible).

In an accountability-based company…

- Each manager has the right span of control to effectively carry out his/her managerial leadership practices.

- Each manager is able to do his/her own work and is not required to "dip down" to fill in for missing roles.

"There is no safety in numbers, or in anything else." (James Thurber, American author, cartoonist, humorist, and satirist, 1894–1961)

T is for three-tier units

Tier (n): two or more rows, levels, or ranks arranged one above another

A three-tier unit is made up of a manager-once-removed, all his/her direct reports, and all their direct reports.

This three-tier unit is a foundation of accountability-based management. It is sometimes called a mutual recognition unit, on the premise that everyone in the unit should at least be able to recognize everyone else.

The most important aspect of three-tier management is that it puts in place a manager-once-removed for all employees—someone those employees can go to for career advice and mentoring, or if they feel unfairly treated by their manager, and someone who makes sure managers carry out their required managerial leadership practices. (See also *Manager*, page 56, and *Manager-once-removed*, page 57.)

In an accountability-based company...

- People understand the concept of three tiers.

- Three-tier meetings take place from time to time.

- Managers-once-removed exercise their unique accountabilities to ensure fairness and equity across the unit.

- Groups of managers-once-removed meet to discuss career opportunities in other three-tier units for their employees-once-removed.

- At a minimum, managers-once-removed know the faces of all people in their three-tier unit.

"If you remember my name, you pay me a subtle compliment; you indicate that I have made an impression on you. Remember my name and you add to my feeling of importance." (Dale Carnegie, American writer and public speaker, 1888–1955)

T is also for timespan of discretion

Span (n):   an extent, stretch, reach, or spread between two limits; a limited space (as of time)

Discretion (n):   ability to make responsible decisions; individual choice or judgment; power of free decision or latitude of choice within certain legal bounds

The timespan of discretion is the length of time a manager grants a direct report to complete a task. During this time the direct report must have the necessary resources (which includes appropriate authority to make whatever decisions are needed). The direct report may "check in" with the manager, keep the manager advised of progress, discuss issues, and obtain advice, but is accountable for getting the task done.

The timespan of discretion of the longest task in a role determines the level (complexity) of work someone is doing. A longer timespan is likely to involve more variables and unknowns, and requires the ability to juggle shorter tasks against the longer one so all work is completed at the right time and to quality standards (see also *Level of work complexity*, page 52). Someone who is given a task with a longer timespan of discretion than he/she can handle will tend to focus on the shorter-term tasks and neglect the longer one until it is too late to successfully complete it. Conversely, someone who is given tasks with very short timespans of discretion but who is capable of handling longer ones will become frustrated and bored, and may start to invent tasks with a timespan that matches his/her own capability.

In an accountability-based company...

- Managers delegate work with an appropriate timespan of discretion for their direct reports.

- Managers provide resources for direct reports to do the work, and do not interfere (but provide advice if asked).

- Managers watch for signs that their direct reports are capable of handling tasks within the designated timespan of discretion, and make adjustments as necessary (breaking larger tasks down into smaller chunks for those who struggle, or discussing with a person's MoR if a person is over-capable and needs to be given some developmental opportunities).

"It takes twenty years to make an overnight success." (Eddie Cantor, American comedian and singer, 1892–1964)

And T is for trust

Trust (n):   assured reliance on the character, ability, strength, or truth of
                        someone or something

An accountability-based workplace is built on trust and the premise
that people can be sure no-one else in the workplace will intentionally
do them harm. Managers and managers-once-removed can promote
trust by being fair and consistent. All employees can promote trust by
being honest in their conversations and sticking to commitments, or
letting people know early if they can no longer do so.

In an accountability-based company...

- People do not intentionally do harm to each other.

- People trust others to do their work to the best of their ability.

- People trust their manager to treat them fairly and equitably.

- People trust their manager-once-removed to look out for their
  career interests.

- People make realistic commitments, and manage those
  commitments impeccably.

"Trust is the lubrication that makes it possible for organizations to work."
(Warren G. Bennis, American psychologist, management educator, and
consultant, 1925–)

U is for under-performance

Performance (n):   the execution of an action; something accomplished

Under (adj):   lower than usual, proper, or desired in amount, quality, or degree

Someone who is under-performing is someone who is not achieving their goals or meeting his/her manager's expectations. It may be because the person is not the right one for the role: perhaps he/she finds the work too complex, does not have the skills and knowledge, or does not value the work. There may be other environmental factors that prevent the person from being successful. Whatever the reason, the individual involved usually knows that he/she is no longer on track and is accountable to tell his/her manager (without fear of reprisal), and the manager is accountable to know how that individual is performing and provide coaching at the right time to help the person improve. If, for some reason, the person cannot improve, the manager is also accountable to discuss the situation with the person's manager-once-removed and initiate removal from role. This doesn't necessarily mean firing the person, but it does mean making all possible efforts to find a better role fit.

In an accountability-based company...

- All efforts are made to place people in roles where they can be successful.

- People feel comfortable approaching their manager to discuss factors that prevent them from being successful.

- Managers are aware of how their direct reports are performing, and discuss performance issues promptly.

- Managers initiate removal from a role if a direct report is the wrong person for the job.

- If someone is not a good fit for their current role, managers-once-removed know of other opportunities across the organization and do their best to place that person appropriately.

"Never promise more than you can perform." (Publilius Syrus, Roman writer of mimes, circa 100 BC)

V is for values

Value (n): something (as a principle or quality) intrinsically valuable or desirable

In accountability-based management terms, values are the norms and boundaries that guide how role holders act. Some commonly stated values are mutual trust, openness, honesty, individual recognition, and customer responsiveness. There are many more.

Values are personal: no company has the right to impose values on its employees, nor to even ask what its employees' values are. For a successful relationship, employees do not need to personally share the company's stated values, but they do need to be able to support them and behave appropriately to demonstrate that support. In other words, the values describe boundaries within which employees must behave, and allow people (from the front line right up to the leader of the organization) to be called to account for not doing so. As an example, a company may expect its employees to demonstrate the following in support of its values:

- Commitment

- Integrity

- Cooperation

- Reliability

- Initiative

- Personal effectiveness

The requirement to demonstrate these should be made clear when employees are hired, and there should be consequences applied to anyone who doesn't demonstrate them, otherwise it becomes obvious that the company's values are something other than what is stated.

It is not a one-way street. Employees who agree to support company values have the right to expect certain things from the company in return. Those things are

- a clearly defined role.

- fulfilling work.

- authority to act.

- a competent manager.

- the opportunity to participate.

- fair treatment.

In an accountability-based company...

- Values are explicitly stated.

- Employee behaviour reflects the company's values.

- People (at any level) can call each other to account for not behaving within the stated values.

"It is a good idea to be ambitious, to have goals, to want to be good at what you do, but it is a terrible mistake to let drive and ambition get in the way of treating people with kindness and decency." (Robert Solow, American economist, 1924–)

W is for work

Work (n): activity in which one exerts strength or faculties to do or perform something; sustained physical or mental effort to overcome obstacles and achieve an objective or result

For people, work is a thinking process that involves using judgment and making decisions to achieve a result or *output*. Doing work usually involves deciding how best to balance pace (how quickly something must be done) against quality (how well). Work becomes more complex if you have to balance one task against others, and if there are more variables or unknown factors to deal with (see also *Information processing capability*, page 39; and *Level of work complexity*, page 52).

For an organization, work is what goes on to support the customer or to support the company itself. Organizational work can be divided into the following categories:

- Mainstream—work that directly supports and satisfies customer needs (selling, marketing, provisioning, development).

- Resource sustainment—providing services and support to ensure effective stewardship of resources (financial, human, material).

- Resource enhancement—significantly changing or improving how mainstream business work is carried out.

- Staff specialist—providing specialty advice to business unit heads and managers.

When designing an organization structure, roles performing work of a similar category should be typically grouped together to minimize coordination costs.

In an accountability-based company...

- People understand that there are different levels of work complexity, and that all levels are equally important.

- People have the right capability to perform the work in their role.

- Work is effectively grouped to meet the organization's mandate while minimizing duplication, cross-functional friction, and the cost/effort of coordination.

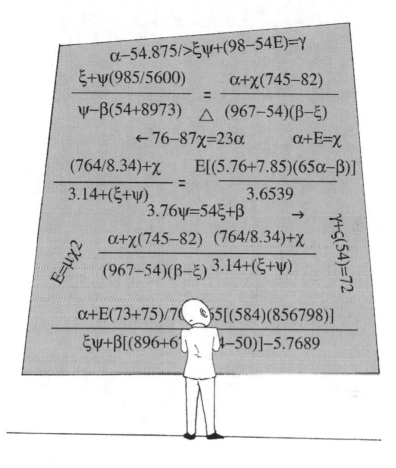

"I think and think for months and years. Ninety-nine times the conclusion is false. The hundredth time I am right." (Albert Einstein, German-born mathematical physicist, 1879–1955)

X is for cross-boundary relationships

Cross (adj):   Lying across or athwart, mutually opposed, involving mutual interchange

Boundary (n):   Something (as a line, point, or plane) that indicates or fixes a limit or extent

Relationship (n): The state of being related or interrelated; a state of affairs existing between those having relations or dealings

Cross-boundary (also *cross-functional*) relationships are those where, in order to do your own work, you need to initiate work with someone who is not your direct report. These working relationships are sometimes called *task initiating role relationships* or TIRRs, to differentiate them from the *task assigning role relationship* (TARR) between a manager and direct report. Because there is no managerial relationship, and therefore the potential for conflicting priorities, cross-boundary relationships need to be clearly defined so the people involved understand what they need and can expect of each other, why, and how to escalate if things go off the rails (see *Escalations*, page 23).

A manager is accountable to define required cross-boundary relationships and authorities for his/her team members. The manager-once-removed is accountable to approve the relationships and deal with any escalated problems. Defining the relationship involves clarifying the circumstances under which the role holders need to work together and the degree of authority each role has:

- Provide advice. (You are accountable to give advice, but the other person does not have to take it.)

- Receive or provide a service (see page 82).

- Monitor for compliance with policies and practices, and for any impacts on work in other areas. (You can try to persuade—but cannot tell—the role holder(s) being monitored to make changes.)

- Coordinate others' work and processes. (You can monitor the work of other role holders involved and can call meetings that the other role holders must attend.)

- Audit to ensure compliance to policies, mandated practices, and legislation. (You can tell a non-compliant role holder to stop doing something.)

- Prescribe a specific course of action. (You can tell someone to do something, and they must do it—usually reserved for high-impact safety issues.)

In an accountability-based company...

- Cross-boundary relationships are clearly defined, with manager and manager-once-removed approval.

- People understand what is expected of them and what authority they have across boundaries.

- People know what to do and who to go to if efforts to resolve cross-boundary issues directly fail, and there is no blame attached to escalation.

"Assumptions are the termites of relationships." (Henry Winkler, American television actor, 1945–)

105

Y is for you

You (pron):   the one or ones being addressed

Whether you're an front-line employee, a manager, a manager-once-removed, or an individual contributor, and whatever your role's level of work complexity, you play an important part in the success of your organization. Remember that in return for providing meaningful work and fair pay, the accountability-based organization expects you to do your best at all times. You can help promote an atmosphere of trust by ensuring no surprises (for your manager or your direct reports), making clear commitments and sticking to them, being fair and equitable in your dealings with others, and generally operating in a spirit of cooperation and teamwork.

In an accountability-based company...

- It's well known that people provide the means of achieving the organization's goals.

- Employees, at all levels, always apply their best efforts to their work.

- People treat others fairly, and with honesty and respect.

- People at all levels are valued for their unique contribution.

"The roots of true achievement lie in the will to become the best that you can become." (Harold Taylor, British architect, 1895–1919)

Z is for ze glossary and ze end

A quick reference for some of the terms that come up regularly in this book:

Employee-once-removed (EoR)	A direct report of your direct report; an employee two levels down.
Gap	A situation where a person does not have a manager performing work at the next highest level of complexity.
Individual contributor	A person who provides specialized knowledge or skills, usually without direct reports.
IPC	Information processing capability—a person's ability to make plans and decisions based on a number of different pieces of information. The more variables involved, the more complex the thinking involved.
Jam-up (also called *compression*)	A situation where a manager and direct report are both performing work at the same level of complexity.
Manager-once-removed (MoR)	Your manager's manager, with unique accountabilities regarding your fair treatment and career development.
Output	Something you produce: the end result of a task.
Role-person fit or role fit	How well a person's information processing capability, knowledge/skills, valuing of the work, and behaviours match those required by a role.
Timespan (of discretion)	The length of time a manager grants a direct report to carry out a particular task.
Level of work complexity (also called *stratum*)	A band of work of a particular complexity. The timespan of discretion of a role's longest task determines the level of work complexity.